# The
# Bible &
# Science
# made easy

*Mark Water*

W0011053

**HENDRICKSON**
PUBLISHERS

***The Bible and Science Made Easy***
Hendrickson Publishers, Inc.
P.O. Box 3473
Peabody, Massachusetts 01961-3473

Copyright © 2001
John Hunt Publishing
Text copyright © 2001 Mark Water

ISBN 1-56563-619-8

Designed and produced
by Tony Cantale Graphics

First printing — October 2001

Manufactured in Hong Kong/China

Photography supplied by
Artville; Digital Stock; Digital
Vision; Goodshoot; Photo Alto;
Photodisc; Ancient Art and
Architecture Collection: G. Torto;
R. Sheridan; T. Walmsley and
Tony Cantale

Illustrations by
Tony Cantale Graphics

# Contents

## Special pull-out chart

The Bible and the cosmos

# The Creator God

### In the beginning

The opening verses of the Bible describe God creating the world.

There is no philosophical argument about: "Does God exist?" The Bible nowhere attempts to "prove" the existence of God. The Bible assumes God's existence. It opens immediately by stating:

**"In the beginning God ..."**
*Genesis 1:1*

### God as Creator

The Bible teaches that God created our universe out of nothing – that he is the Creator of all human life. Genesis asserts:

**"God created man
in his own image,
in the image of God
he created him;
male and female
he created them."**
*Genesis 1:27*

4

### God is called Creator

The title, Creator, is given to God in several places in the Bible.

> "Remember your Creator."
> *Ecclesiastes 12:1*

> "They exchanged the truth of God for a lie, and worshiped and served created things rather than the Creator—who is for ever praised. Amen."
> *Romans 1:25*

> "Do you not know?
> Have you not heard?
> The Lord is the everlasting God, the Creator of the ends of the earth."
> *Isaiah 40:28*

### God's purpose in creation

Why did God create the world and everything that lives in it? It's not really possible to think of God existing if he could not express:

- **his creative power**
  > "For by him [God] all things were created: things in heaven and on earth, visible and invisible, whether thrones or powers or rulers or authorities; all things were created by him and for him."
  > *Colossians 1:15-16*

- **his authority and wisdom**
  > "But God made the earth by his power;
  > he founded the world by his wisdom
  > and stretched out the heavens by his understanding."
  > *Jeremiah 10:11-12*

- **his love**
  > "I provide [for] ... the people I formed for myself that they may proclaim my praise."
  > *Isaiah 43:20-21*

  > "I have loved you with an everlasting love;
  > I have drawn you with loving-kindness."
  > *Jeremiah 31:3*

# The argument from design

## The teleological argument

The teleological argument for the existence of God comes from the Greek word telos meaning "purpose" or "goal". Teleology is the study of goals or ends. It focuses on:

• the evidence of design in our world
• the evidence of purpose in our world

The teleological argument, while not able to "prove" the existence of God, demonstrates that there are countless pointers in our world which make it reasonable to conclude that the world exists because of a Creator God.

This argument confirms the most basic Christian belief about God creating the world, that, in the words of Genesis 2:4: **"The Lord God made the earth and the heavens."**

## The watchmaker argument

The teleological argument is illustrated by the watchmaker argument. The theologian William Paley (1743–1805) made this argument well

known. If we were to find a watch lying on a beach, we would probably not assume that it just evolved out of the sand. We would rightly conclude that it had been made by an intelligent designer and somehow transported to that particular spot.

We would never infer in the case of a mechanism such as a watch that its design was due to natural processes such as the wind and rain; rather, the existence of a watch points to the probability of a watchmaker.

Living things are similar to mechanisms, exhibiting the same sort of orderly complexity, and we must therefore infer by analogy that their design is also the result of intelligent activity.

## Beauty and variety

The beauty of our world and the amazing variety within our world have convinced countless people, scientists and non-scientists alike, that there must be a Designer behind our universe.

### The cosmological

The cosmologica for the existence from the Greek w meaning world or states that everyth exists must have a "First Cause". Nothing that we observe in the world today was produced by itself.

This argument concludes that there must have been an infinite, un-caused "First Cause" or "Prime Mover" who initiated a chain of secondary causes and effects. We assume

of the universe and the wonder of creation point to an infinite creator God.

### The teaching of the Bible

The Bible categorically states that the world around us points to God.

**"The heavens proclaim his [God's] righteousness."**
*Psalm 50:6*

# The God of the gaps (1)

### God speaks through nature

Psalm 19 tells us that God speaks to us through nature which includes the numerous scientific wonders of the world.

> **"The heavens declare the glory of God;**
> **the skies proclaim the work of his hands.**
> **Day after day they pour forth speech;**
> **night after night they display knowledge."**
> *Psalm 19:1-2*

### Scientific knowledge

Some scientists argue that humans no longer need to believe in God since science has explained away our need. These scientists reason that since we have "come of age", having understood more about our world, we can shed old religious ideas. The world's first astronaut, Yuri Gagarin, held this view as he declared on April 12, 1961, that he had not seen God in the space above the sky – implying that this proved that God did not exist.

### Is belief in God needed in the 21st century?

It has been calculated that the temperature at the core of the sun is about 15,000,000°C, and the pressure is equal to that of 400,000 million atmospheres. This gives rise to nuclear fusion in which atoms of hydrogen combine to form helium. This is the type of reaction that is used to make a hydrogen bomb.

Instead of allowing these facts to increase a sense of awe and wonder at the power of God who can create such power, some scientists use the discovery of such mechanisms as an excuse to deny the existence of the Creator – "If life and the universe occur naturally: why do we need God?".

The 18th-century astronomer Pierre Laplace explained nature as a self-sufficient mechanism. "As for God," he told Emperor Napoleon, "I have no need of that hypothesis."

(Note: Naturalism is the belief that nature is explained solely by the laws of chemistry and physics.)

## What is the "God of the gaps" theory?

It is the belief that the working of God can be seen in those things which science cannot explain.

The disparaging phrase, "God of the gaps" is used to describe a rather weak version of God who stands in for some missing piece of scientific knowledge. So God might currently be invoked to explain such things as consciousness. Every scientific advance reduces the room given to this "God of the gaps".

## The Bible and the God of the gaps

Science may find a mechanism to "explain" some substance, item, or entity, but the Scriptures know nothing of a God who fills the slots in the gaps of our scientific understanding. A man or woman of science who is also a Christian finds each new scientific discovery about our world a source of enrichment. They stand in wonder at God's marvelous work.

## God is the Prime Cause

The Bible states that God is the Prime Cause of all things.

> **"Yet for us there is but one God, the Father, from whom all things came and for whom we live; and there is but one Lord, Jesus Christ, through whom all things came and through whom we live."** *1 Corinthians 8:6*

## The God of grace is the God of nature

Christians are not (or at least, should not be) frightened by truth. Wherever truth is found Christians should rejoice. They welcome truth, even when it is "discovered" by a scientific humanist. They believe that truth is part of God's self-disclosure.

# The God of the gaps (2)

### Rejection of God

Scientists limit the sphere of activity to what they are researching. They are not trying to determine whether or not the world is here for a purpose. Concepts such as "purpose" and "God" lie outside the scope of science. Many scientists conclude that God either does not exist or is unimportant as far as science is concerned.

### Error

The cardinal error in the "God of the gaps" theory is the claim that there is room for God only in the areas where man's knowledge has yet to reach.

### The God of the Bible

The one characteristic that the God of the Bible does not possess is that of being God of the gaps.

### God is immanent

The Bible teaches that God is everywhere. He upholds every part of his universe.

> "In him all things hold together." *Colossians 1:17*

### God is beyond humankind's imagination

The Bible teaches that God transcends even our very best thoughts about him.

> "God ... alone is immortal and ... lives in unapproachable light, whom no one has seen or can see." *1 Timothy 6:15-16*

### God and the world

God does not have the kind of relationship to the world that a mechanic has to a machine. The Bible teaches that God has an intimate relationship with the world.

He is the One who holds the whole universe in being "By his word of power," says Hebrews 1:3.

> "In him we live and move and have our being." *Acts 17:28*

> "since he himself gives to all men life and breath and everything." *Acts 17:25*

> "Every single thing was created through, and for, him. He is both the first principle and the upholding principle of the whole scheme of creation." *Colossians 1:16, 17, J. B. Phillips*

> "We are indeed his offspring." *Acts 17: 29*

## "Thinking God's thoughts after him"

John Kepler (1571–1630) revolutionized the astronomical thinking of his day by disproving the accepted view that there were only circular movements among the heavenly bodies. He observed the 8 degrees of divergence from the circular in the orbit of Mars. All other astronomers believed that the planets and stars had a circular obit. But Kepler had such respect for the world that God had made, the actual world as he observed it, that he would not deny his observations. He published them, even though it meant that many regarded him as a heretic.

## Kepler's Christian beliefs

Kepler insisted that the universe itself was an expression of the being of God. When he did his scientific study, Kepler said that he felt himself to be "thinking God's thoughts after him." He said that he was "religiously bound to alter not one jot or tittle of what it had pleased God to write down in nature."

## The grandeur of God

Scientific discoveries are constantly revealing the wonders of our physical world. For Christians these amazing discoveries show us more of the grandeur of God.

# Look at the birds

**The wonders of nature speak of God**
"Every creature is a divine word because it proclaims God." *Bonaventura*

### Feathers
Throughout the animal kingdom only birds have feathers. Emperor penguins have as many as 30,000 feathers, while tiny hummingbirds (the best fliers) have only about 1,000.

**Emperor penguin**

## Hummingbirds

### Wing-beat rate
The largest hummingbird, the Giant Hummingbird, has a wing-beat rate of 10-15 wing-beats per second.

The fastest recorded wing-beat rate is 80 per second, by a tiny Amethyst Woodstar. The slightly smaller Bee Hummingbird – the world's smallest bird – may have an even faster rate. The Ruby-throated Hummingbird averages around 53 wing-beats per second in normal flight.

**Ruby-throated hummingbird**

### Plumage and Colors
The brilliant, iridescent colors of hummingbird plumage are caused by the refraction of light produced by the structures of certain feathers. Like any diffraction grating or prism, these structures split light into its component colors, and only certain frequencies are refracted back to the viewer.

The apparent color of any particular part of a feather depends upon the distance between the microscopic ridges in its grid-like structure. The resulting colors are much more vivid and iridescent than those of birds with only pigmented feathers.

Iridescent hummingbird colors are formed by a combination of refraction and pigmentation, since the diffraction structures themselves are made of melanin, a pigment.

## Wing-beats
**Bird wing-beats per second**

| | |
|---|---|
| Robin | 2 |
| Pigeon | 3 |
| Chickadee | 27 |
| Hummingbird | 10–80 |

## Wondering eyes
Happy is he and more than wise
Who sees with wondering eyes and clean
The world through all the grey disguise
Of sleep and custom in between.

*G.K. Chesterton*

## Building blocks
When we consider the incredible complexity and variety of the world around us, we are filled with a sense of wonder. The facts we see and hear are building blocks to this end.

The intricacies of individual birds' feathers, the amazing rate of the humming bird's wing-beat and dazzling colors of their plumage all speak volumes about the heavenly Designer of every creature in the animal kingdom.

## All animal life is from God
The book of Job states unequivocally that all animal life, as well as all human life, is from God.

**"In his hand is the life of every creature and the breath of all mankind."** *Job 12:10*

# Eagles

### The way of an eagle
"There are three things that are too amazing for me, four that I do not understand: the way of an eagle in the sky ..."
*Proverbs 30:18-19*

All beauty in nature and the stunning variety of animals and birds in the animal kingdom lead Christians to worship the Creator God who created all life in the beginning and continues to sustain all life today.

## The Bald Eagle

### Name
The word "bald" originally meant "white-headed." The scientific name, *Haliaeetus leucocephalus*, means "white headed sea eagle".

### Quick facts

**Size:** With a 6.5- to 7-foot wingspan, the bald eagle is one of the largest birds of prey in the world. The adult eagle is 3–3.5 feet tall.

**Longevity:** Although the life expectancy of wild eagles may be 30 years, some have lived 50 years in captivity.

**Eyesight:** The bald eagle's eyesight is 5 to 6 times sharper than a human's.

**Speed:** Eagles fly 20 to 60 miles per hour in normal flight and dive at more than 100 miles an hour.

**Food:** Fish eater

### Differences from the golden eagle
The bald eagle's legs are naked, while golden eagles have feathers all the way down to the talons. In flight, bald eagles soar with flat wings while golden eagles soar with their wings raised in a slight "V".

### Nests
Bald eagles usually built their nests near the top of a large tree. Enlarged annually, a bald eagle's nest can become the largest of any North American bird's. The record nest measured 20 feet deep, 10 feet wide and weighed two tons!

### Eagle-eyed vision

The color vision of eagles is superior to that of humans. Human eyes have pigments in their cones which are sensitive to red, blue and green light. Eagles have not only these three visual pigments but also an extra two.

### The eagles' built-in sunglasses

Some eagles possess eye filters which cut out the sunlight's glare, just as Polaroid sunglasses do.

### All living creatures

The very name "creature" reminds us that all living beings are created by God, the Creator. The word "creature" comes from the Latin word creatura, meaning "thing created." The dictionary definition of "creature" is "a created being." We should talk about living creatures – not living things. Animals and birds are all God's creatures. The power and speed of an eagle's flight should turn our thoughts to the eagle's Creator.

### The Psalmist praises our Creator God

When the Psalmist looked at the sky he was reminded that nobody can be compared to God.

> "The heavens praise your wonders, O Lord. . . . For who in the skies above can compare with the Lord?" Psalm 89:5-6

The Psalmist gave thanks to God for everything in creation, because God had and continues to create every living creature.

> "The heavens are yours, and yours also the earth; you founded the world and all that is in it." Psalm 89:11

So, we don't simply look at a bald eagle and merely say, "What a magnificent bird." We must also say, "How wonderful is God, who created such a magnificent bird."

### Louis Pasteur

Louis Pasteur, the French chemist who founded modern microbiology and invented the process of pasteurization, once said, **"The more I study nature, the more I am amazed at the Creator."**

# Look at the butterflies and the moths

## Butterfly migration

The most famous migrating butterfly is the North American Monarch Butterfly. Unlike most other insects in temperate climates, Monarch butterflies cannot survive a long cold winter. Instead, they spend the winter in roosting spots. At the end of summer all the Monarch butterflies in Canada and Central America fly south, often, as far as 1,750 miles. They travel on fixed flight paths, up to 20 miles per hour, to a few selected forests in Mexico. There millions of them hang on the trees, often the same trees each year. These forests have a high humidity so the butterflies are in no danger of drying out, and the temperature seldom varies, never going below freezing point. As soon as spring arrives the Monarchs retrace their long journey back to North America.

### A unique migration

The Monarchs of North America travel much farther than all other tropical butterflies and are the only butterflies to make such a long, two-way migration every year.

### An astonishing phenomenon

**"The migration of the Monarchs is and remains an astonishing phenomenon in the world of butterflies."** *Wijbren Landman, in Butterfly Encyclopaedia.*

## Moths

### The Atlas moth

The female Atlas moth produces a chemical "messenger" called a *pheromone* when it wants to attract a male moth. The male moth, using its very large antennae, can detect the female moth's scent in the air more than four miles away.

### The Polyphemus moth

The larva of the Polyphemus moth consumes over 86,000 times its own body weight by the time it is eight weeks old.

### Defense mechanisms of the moth

The Blue Underwing Moth has ears on the sides of its wings that helps it to hear the squeaks of bats. If it hears a bat coming, it will drop to the ground or dodge out of the way.

### The Red Underwing Moth,

if disturbed by an enemy, opens and closes its wings so that the bright flashes of red frighten the enemy.

### The Christian perspective

Christians have no doubt about their response to the question: "Is this migration by happenstance?" They would say that built into the Monarch butterfly there is a navigation trigger and navigation guide and map, designed by a Master Navigator, by God himself.

### Looking beyond nature

The wonders of the animal kingdom direct us to the Creator of the birds and the bees and all other creatures. Incandescent butterfly wings should raise our thoughts to the all-powerful, most-creative, heavenly Designer who created and "designed" every insect that ever lived.

The English poet, William Cowper, articulated his sense of awe and wonder toward the Creator of all animals and the whole of nature, when he wrote: **"Nature is but a name for an effect whose cause is God."**

### God created the butterflies and the moths

Moths, butterfly, and all insects are included in what the Psalmist calls "creatures" made by God.

> **"How many are your works, O Lord!**
> **In wisdom you made them all; the earth is full of your creatures."** Psalm 104:24

# Science in the Bible (1)

## Writing off the Bible

For many years, critics have claimed that the Bible is full of scientific inaccuracies and errors reflecting the naiveté of the ancient biblical authors.

Others, including some who profess to be Christians, argue that since the Bible is a religious book, it need not be accurate in matters of science or history. Such critics have concluded that when the Bible speaks about scientific matters, it can be interpreted spiritually or allegorically instead of literally.

## Astronomy

Before the invention of the telescope some of the references to stars in the Bible must have appeared to be exaggerating.

> The angel of the Lord called to Abraham ... "I will surely bless you and make your descendants as numerous as the stars in they sky and as the sand on the seashore."
> *Genesis 22: 15, 17*

> "I will make the descendants of David ... as countless as the stars of the sky."
> *Jeremiah 33:22*

## Counting the stars

Men have always been fascinated by the stars and many have tried to count them. Ptolemy came up with 1,056. Tycho Brahe counted 777. Johannes found 1,005.

If one counts every star that is visible from every point on the globe, the maximum number of stars that may be seen by the naked eye is around 4,000, But 4,000 is certainly not a "countless" number, and certainly not a number to be compared to the number of grains of sand on the sea shore.

## A universe that cannot be measured

The prophet Jeremiah implies that the universe itself cannot be measured.

> "This is what the Lord says:
> 'Only if the heavens above can be measured
> and the foundations of the earth below be searched out
> will I reject all the descendants of Israel
> because of all they have done ...'"
> *Jeremiah 31:37*

Even today, with our sophisticated telescopes, this biblical statement is still true.

### The telescope

With the invention of the telescope came the discovery of countless more stars. Scientists now estimate that the universe contains at least $10^{26}$ stars (that is 100,000,000,000,000,000, 000,000,000), which is a number that reflects the same order of magnitude as the number of grains of sand on the earth.

### Every star differs from all other stars

"The sun has one kind of splendor, the moon another and the stars another; and star differs from star in splendor."
*1 Corinthians 15:41*

For centuries this idea seemed like a mistake since so many stars appeared to be the same. But modern astronomical observations declare that no two stars are alike.

### Named

"'To whom will you compare me?
Or who is my equal?'" says the Holy One.
Lift your eyes and look to the heavens.
Who created all these?
He who brings out the starry host one by one,
and calls them by name.
Because of his great power and mighty strength,
not one of them is missing."
*Isaiah 40:25-26*

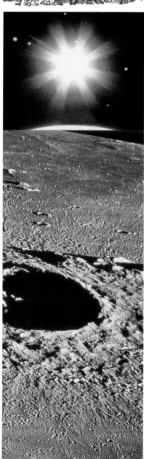

# Science in the Bible (2)

### What if the Bible had scientific mistakes in it?

The Bible is not primarily a history book nor is the Bible a book about science. The Bible claims to be the inspired word of God. If it is not what it claims to be, then it cannot be trusted in matters of theology, much less science and history.

But, if the Bible is what it claims to be, then it cannot contain errors of any kind.

### The accuracy of the Bible in scientific matters

We must, therefore, conclude that although the Bible is not primarily a science book, it is nevertheless accurate when its intention is to speak on matters of history and science; and it is always truthful.

### Poetry and the Bible

The Book of Psalms and many passages throughout the Bible use poetic language. Poets employ metaphor, simile, hyperbole and other figures of speech to communicate the truth of what they are saying (see also pages 50–51). When we look for the "accuracy" of a statement we need to examine both the purpose and the type or style of writing. For example, in Revelation, John speaks of the Lamb on the throne (Revelation 7:9) but he did not mean a literal lamb.

### Different language, same message

The Bible does not use modern scientific terminology, but this has never prevented it from speaking about basic scientific principles in everyday language.

### Biology

The circulation of blood was not discovered until 1616, yet thousands of years before William Harvey's great discovery, the Bible said:

**"For the life of a creature is in the blood."** *Leviticus 17:11*

Only recently has modern biology been able to investigate the amazing properties of blood. Before that we did not fully appreciate the accuracy of this verse in Leviticus. We now know that the cells of the body depend upon the blood to supply the food, water, and oxygen that they must have to survive. Life truly is in the blood.

### The water cycle

The Bible has many references to the field of hydrology, the "science of water." It refers to the cycle of water which is the well-known process by which water vapor is condensed and falls as rain or snow. The water is then drained off the land through a system of streams and rivers, until it eventually reaches the sea, when it is returned to the skies through evaporation.

> **"All streams flow into the sea,
> yet the sea is never full.
> To the place the streams come from,
> there they return again."**
> *Ecclesiastes 1:7*

> **"As the rain and the snow
> come down from heaven,
> and do not return to it
> without watering the earth
> and making it bud and flourish,
> so that it yields seed for the sower and bread for the eater,
> so is my word that goes out from my mouth."**
> *Isaiah 55:10*

This is significant because the water cycle was not demonstrated scientifically until recent times.

### Scientific explanations

The Bible neither denies nor plays down the scientific level of explanation.

> **"The Lord God formed man from the dust of the ground."**
> *Genesis 2:7*

> **"The Lord drove the sea back with a strong east wind and turned it into dry land."**
> *Exodus 14:21*

# Medicine and health

### The Mosaic Law

The laws given by God to Moses show a keen awareness of hygiene and health requirements.

## Quarantine for people with infectious diseases

"When anyone has a swelling or a rash or a bright spot on his skin that may become an infectious skin disease, he must be brought to Aaron the priest ... If the spot on his skin is white but does not appear to be more than skin deep and the hair in it has not turned white, the priest is to put the infected person in isolation for seven days." *Leviticus 13:2, 4*

## How to set up latrines hygienically

"Designate a place outside the camp where you can go to relieve yourself. As part of your equipment have something to dig with, and when you relieve yourself, dig a hole and cover up your excrement."
*Deuteronomy 23:12-13*

## Special cleansing after touching the dead

"Whoever touches the dead body of anyone will be unclean for seven days. He must purify himself with the water on the third day and on the seventh day; then he will be clean."
*Numbers 19:11-12*

If the health and hygiene laws given Israel by Moses had been obeyed by Europeans in the Middle Ages many of the plagues that ravaged Europe would have not occurred.

## The ban on eating unclean animals

Some Bible scholars say that the rules for eating clean and unclean food were originally given for health reasons. Whatever the reason, modern research shows that:

• **Eating certain fish can be dangerous**
Fish without fins and scales were "unclean" and not to be eaten.
"... anything that does not have fins and scales you may not eat; for you it is unclean."
*Deuteronomy 14:10*
Today we know that shell fish and crustaceans carry disease and can easily cause food poisoning.

• **Eating pork can be dangerous**
Pork was not to be eaten.
"The pig is also unclean ..."
*Deuteronomy 14:8*
We now know that meat from swine can cause illness.

## Stress

Doctors now agree that anxiety, stress, and anger contribute to many illnesses. This was known to the wisdom writers.

"A cheerful heart is good medicine,
but a crushed spirit dries up the bones." Proverbs 17:22

"A heart at peace gives life to the body,
but envy rots the bones."
*Proverbs 14:30*

## Created bodies

The God who made the human body knows what is needed to keep the body whole, healthy, and at peace – and the laws given in the Bible show this.

# Look at the fish

## Teeming with creatures
"There is the sea, vast and
spacious,
teeming with creatures beyond
number–
living things both large and
small."
*Psalm 104:25*

## Holding one's breath
• Humans can only hold their
breath under water for about
2 minutes.
• Penguins can stay
underwater for up to 15
minutes.
• Sperm whales can stay
underwater for over 90
minutes before having to
surface for fresh air.

## God's provision for Jonah
"But the Lord provided a great
fish to swallow Jonah, and
Jonah was inside the fish three
days and three nights."
*Jonah 1:17*

## Mormyrids
Mormyrids, fish which live in
slow-moving rivers, have an
ability shared by few other
creatures. They navigate by
using their electrical sense.
Their tails give out so many
pulses of electricity that they
can create an electrical field
around themselves. When any
object in the water disturbs
this electrical field, receptors in
the head pick up the signals.

## Whales

### The blue whale – the largest animal
The blue whale is the largest
living animal, weighing up to 169
tons (the equivalent weight of
thirty elephants) and growing to
110 feet long.

### The humpback whale
Named for the distinctive hump
behind the dorsal fin, this is an
agile and acrobatic whale, often
leaping out of the water and
slapping its tail and flippers on
the water. The most amazing
characteristic of the humpback is
its song – a fascinating pattern of
grunts, squeals, squeaks, moans
and hums in repeated sequences
that may go on for 20 minutes or
more.

In Antarctic waters
humpback whales congregate
during the summer months to
feed on krill (phosphorescent
shrimps), each whale eating
about one ton of krill a day.

### The sperm whale
Humans are unable to dive lower
than 400 feet in water. Beyond
that depth the pressure is too
great. Sperm whales can dive to
depths of greater than 2,700 feet.

### Biggest eyes

The Giant squid has the largest eyes of all animals. Each eyes is 16 inches across and has more than 1,000 million light-sensitive cells.

### Salmon migration

Some adult salmon, when they are ready to mate, travel over 3,000 miles across open seas to the precise stream in which they were born. Scientists believe that they are able to sense the unique chemical "signature" of the stream of water in which they first swam.

### The sea is God's

"The sea is his [God's], for he made it." *Psalm 95:5*

### Conclusion

The point is that seas and rivers are full of myriads of wonders of the world. We sometimes call them the wonders of nature. More accurately we should refer to them as the wonders of our Creator God. He, and he alone, was totally responsible for the creation of water, seas, rivers and the earth in the first place, as well as all of today's rivers, lakes, and seas with their teeming fish.

A sperm whale displays his flukes.

# Science is not against the Bible

## Modern science and Christianity

In the sixteenth and seventeenth centuries modern science flourished in the center of a growing Christian civilization in Europe. Science was not seen as a challenge to the Bible and neither did Christianity oppose science.

## Royal Society

The world-renowned Royal Society, founded by Britain's leading scientists in the seventeenth century, dedicated their efforts "to the glory of God the Creator, and the benefit of the human race."

## Scientists and Christianity today

Professor Arnold Wolfendale, upon being appointed Astonomer Royal in England, declared in 1991, "I think the hand of God can be seen everywhere."

Far from all scientists being atheists, many believe in God. The Research Scientists' Christian Fellowship has 700 members in Britain, and its sister fellowship on America has over 2,000 members.

**"The more that astronomers learn about the origin and development of the universe, the more evidence they accumulate for the God of the Bible."** *Hugh Ross, Ph.D.*

## Scientists and Christianity

Many of the early scientists were deeply committed Christians.

**Francis Bacon** (1561-1626) saw God's works in nature and his words in the Bible as the twin facets of his self-disclosure.

**Isaac Newton** (1642–1727) has been called "the greatest scientist of all time."

**Robert Boyle** (1627–91) "the father of modern chemistry" and famous for his Boyle's Law.

**Michael Faraday** (1701–1867) a pioneer in the field of electro-magneticism. We owe most of the basic discoveries in electricity to Christian believers. Faraday was arguably the greatest experimental scientist of all time.

**Gregor Mendel** (1822–84) pioneered early work about genetics and was the Abbot of a monastery.

## Integrity

The fact that many scientists are Christians does not, in itself, prove that Christianity is true. It does show, though, that Christianity and science are not incompatible. Both can be trusted with total integrity. There is no competition between Christianity and science.

## Testimony from a non-Christian scientist

The incredible complexity of life at the microbiological level arouses a feeling of awe in all. A leading (non-Christian) molecular biologist, writes:

"Is it really credible that random processes could have constructed a reality, the smallest element of which – a functional protein or gene – is complex beyond our own creative capacities, a reality which is the very antithesis of chance, which excels in every sense anything produced by the intelligence of man? Alongside the level of ingenuity and complexity exhibited by the molecular machinery of life, even our most advanced artifacts appear clumsy. We feel humbled, as neolithic man in the presence of twentieth-century technology."
*Michael Denton*

## Collaborators

"Some scientists see the scientific quest for knowledge about and understanding our world – and a religious, Christian and biblical faith as collaborators and allies, rather than, and not, enemies and opponents."
*John Young in Teach Yourself Christianity*

# Archaeology affirms the accuracy of the Old Testament

### Archaeology and the Bible

The science of archaeology has proved to be a very valuable tool in better understanding, confirming, and verifying the accuracy of the Bible.

Before the nineteenth century very little was known about the events, background, and setting of the Old and New Testament Scriptures. It was nearly impossible to confirm the reliability of the Biblical record. Modern archaeology, time and again, has provided evidence of the reliability of the Bible.

"As a matter of fact, however, it may be stated categorically that no archaeological discovery has ever controverted a Biblical reference."
*Nelson Gleuck, archaeologist.*

### Testimony from leading biblical archaeologists concerning the Old Testament

"There can be no doubt that archaeology has confirmed the substantial historicity of Old Testament tradition."
*William F. Albright*

"It is therefore legitimate to say that, in respect of that part of the Old Testament against

### Archaeological evidences for the reliability of the Old Testament

"Old Testament archaeology has rediscovered whole nations, resurrected important peoples, and in a most astonishing manner filled in historical gaps, adding immeasurably to the knowledge of Biblical backgrounds." *Merrill Unger*

The great value of archaeology has been to show that the geography, technology, political and military movements, cultures, religious practices, social institutions, languages, customs, and other aspects of everyday life of Israel and other nations of antiquity were exactly as described in the Bible.

**The Black Stele**
Before the impact of biblical archaeology, one of the "assured results of higher criticism" was that the Pentateuch could not have been written by Moses because writing was not yet in existence in Moses' day. These critics assured us that the first five books of the Bible were put together centuries after Moses by a group of editors and were subsequently attributed to Moses.

However, in 1901 the "Black Stele" was found which contained the detailed laws of Hammurabi's Code. The significant aspect of this find was which the disintegrating criticism of the last half of the nineteenth century was chiefly directed, the evidence of archaeology has been to re-establish its authority, and likewise to augment its value by rendering it more intelligible through a fuller knowledge of its background and setting."

*Sir Frederic Kenyon*

**Excavations in the ancient city of Ebla, Syria.**

that it was pre-Mosaic by at least three centuries.

Therefore, it proved that both writing and law codes were in existence centuries before Moses!

## Ebla Tablets

Another archaeological find that confirms the existence of writing centuries before the time of Moses is the discovery of the Ebla Tablets in northern Syria in the 1960's. The Ebla kingdom was in existence approximately 1,000 years before Moses lived.

These documents, written on clay tablets in approximately 2,300 BC, demonstrate that both personal and place names that occur in the account of the patriarchs are genuine.

Critics thought that the name "Canaan" was incorrectly used in the book of Genesis, but it is found in the Ebla Tablets.

The word for "the deep" found in Genesis 1:2 – *tehom* – was said to belong to a time much later that the writing of Genesis. But the word *tehom* also appears in the Ebla Tablets.

# Archaeology affirms the accuracy of the New Testament

### Sir William Ramsay

Sir William Ramsay was one of the greatest archaeologists of modern times, undertaking extensive archaeological work in Asia Minor (modern Turkey). Initially, he started this work as an unbeliever who was thoroughly convinced that the book of Acts was the product of the second century and not written by Luke, a first-century historian. One of his goals was to prove that the history of the first century was inaccurate.

His beliefs were drastically changed when his archaeological finds confirmed the accuracy of the book of Acts in even its minutest detail.

### Acts 14:6

**"But they found out about it [a Jewish plot against Paul and Barnabas] and fled to the Lycaonian cities of Lystra and Derbe and to the surrounding country."** *Acts 14:6*

In the nineteenth century, Acts 14:6 was consistently presented as an example of a historical error. The verse portrays Paul and Barnabas as entering the province of Lycaonia when they came to Lystra and Derbe. The problem was that Iconium, the city from which they had fled, was also in the province of Lycaonia.

Ramsay checked out this passage in his quest to prove the historical inaccuracy of Acts. His archaeological discoveries showed that Iconium was made a part of Phrygia only during AD 37–72: both before and after this it was part of Lycaonia.

Thus we find that Luke's statement was written in the one and only period of history in which it would be accurate!

### The birth of Jesus

Luke was thought also to be totally inaccurate regarding details surrounding the birth of Christ (Luke 2:1-3). Critics argued that Quirinius was governor of Syria at a later date and therefore did not conduct a census at this time. Moreover, it is said that citizens did not have to return to their homelands.

Yet archaeological findings show:
• the Romans held censuses every 14 years.
• Quirinius was governor of Syria twice: in AD 6–9, and also in 6–4 BC. This would correspond to the date of

the census of Luke 2, since it is now thought that Jesus was born in Bethlehem in 6 or 5 BC.

A piece of papyrus found in Egypt details an account where everyone is commanded to report to their home-town for a census. This dates from a century later than the Luke 2 census, but there is now no reason to doubt the accuracy of Luke.

### Pontius Pilate

In 1962, two Italian archaeologists dug up a Latin inscription in the town of Caesarea that read:

> **"Pontius Pilate, Prefect of Judea, has presented the Tiberium to the Caesareans."**

### Herod's temple

In Acts 21:28-31 Paul is (falsely) accused of bringing Greeks into the temple area and so defiling that holy place.

> **"The whole city was aroused, and the people came running from all directions. Seizing Paul, they dragged him from the temple, and immediately the gates were shut."** *Acts 21:31*

In 1871, and again in 1935, signs which forbade non-Jews from entering into the court of the Jews were dug up in Jerusalem.

The stones read:

> **"No alien may enter within the balustrade and enclosure around the sanctuary. Whoever is caught will render himself liable to the death penalty, which will inevitably follow."**

**Stone from the Jerusalem Temple – inscription forbidding entrance by non-Jews to the Temple at the time of Christ.**

### Conclusion

Archaeology continues to show the Bible to be reliable and completely accurate.

# The "Why?" question and the "How?" question

## Two levels of explanation

There are two levels of explanation about our universe.

- There is the scientific investigation and explanation.
- There is the explanation that the Creator God is behind everything in his creation.

Christianity and science are similar in that they both tell us things about our world. Science tells the "How" of God's creation. But God speaks even more clearly in the Bible – giving us the "Why."

## Purpose alongside cause and effect

Christianity says that the universe was created and is sustained by the will of a loving God.

In contrast science does not set out to find out about any purpose that might be behind the world. It is only interested in the cause and effect which makes our world tick. Science is concerned with the rational exploration of what is the case.

## The mechanistic approach

Mechanistic thinking has proved overwhelmingly useful in physics, chemistry, and biology. The recent spectacular progress in molecular biology further attests to the value of a mechanistic approach to humanity.

The Christian, on the other hand, happily accepts that the complexity of life comes from God.

## How? And Why?

"Science tells us how cosmic history started and how it has progressed; theology is concerned with asserting that there has been a mind and purpose behind the process. Two different kinds of issue are involved for science and religion respectively (in simple terms, How? And Why?), which cannot be in conflict with each other."
*John Polkinghorne, President of Queens' College, Cambridge.*

## Science is incomplete

- the awareness of beauty
- the power of music to move the emotions
- the wonder and force of love
- the knowledge of right and wrong
- the outrage we all feel when we hear of human atrocities

These have convinced myriads of people, scientists and non-scientists alike, that there is more to the world than the movements of atoms and molecules.

Even the most learned know there are dimensions of valid human experience not covered by scientific explanation.

## Mystery

"Shall we live in mystery, and yet conduct ourselves as though everything were known?"
*Spoken by Moses in* The Firstborn *by Christopher Fry*

# Look at the insects

## Strongest creature

The rhinoceros beetle, which grows nearly seven inches long, lays claim to being the strongest creature. It can withstand over 800 times its own weight being placed on its back.

## The honey factory

Honey is "manufactured" in one of the world's most efficient factories, the beehive.

To make one pound of honey, bees may travel as far as 55,000 miles and visit more than two million flowers to gather the nectar.

### The variety and value of honey

There are over 300 kinds of honey in the United States. This variety is caused by the diverse floral sources which range from clover to eucalyptus to orange blossom.

Not only has honey been used as a sweetening agent from the earliest of times it has now been found to contain numerous so-called "health foods":
• fructose
• glucose
• trace enzymes
• minerals
• vitamin and
• amino acids.

### A second use of the honey bee

The expression "as busy as a bee" is apt. For a honey bees' wings stroke 11,400 times per minute. In addition to gathering nectar to produce honey, honey bees perform a vital second function – pollination.

About one-third of the human diet is derived from insect-pollinated plants and honey bees are responsible for 80% of this pollination.

### The amazing queen bee

The queen bee is the only sexually developed female in the hive.
• A two-day-old larva is selected by the workers to be reared as the queen. She emerges from her cell 11 days later to mate in flight with as many as 18 drone bees.
• During this mating, she receives several million sperm cells, which last her entire life span of nearly two years.
• The queen starts to lay eggs about 10 days after mating. A productive queen can lay 3,000 eggs in a single day.

### The comb

Honey bees produce a wax comb. The hexagonal design of

the comb has been replicated in constructing the wings of the latest aircraft.

Although the comb's hexagon-shaped walls are only two thousandths of an inch thick, they can bear 25 times their own weight.

### God's doing

Almost everyone marvels when the incredible intricacies of a bee's beehive are pointed out. But the Christian not only admires the cleverness of the bees, he or she stands in awe of the heavenly Designer who created the bees in the first place. Like the psalmist, they want to affirm God's greatness:

> "Great are the works of the Lord." *Psalm 111:2*

Far from being mere quirks of fate each bee is viewed as the amazing creation of the God of creation.

### The Cavendish laboratory

> "The works of the Lord are great, sought out of all them that have pleasure therein." *Psalm 111:2 King James Version*.

The above quotation is inscribed over the entrance to the Cavendish laboratory in Cambridge. The Cavendish Laboratory, opened in 1873, is Cambridge university's famous research center of experimental physics. It has had many of the world's most outstanding physicists on its faculty.

# The universe as a fit habitat

### God as Designer
God designed the universe in such a way that it would support human beings.

"For this is what the Lord says—
he who created the heavens,
he is God;
he who fashioned and made the earth,
he founded it;
he did not create it empty,
but formed it to be inhabited."
*Isaiah 45:18*

### Facing the facts
Scientists emphasize the need for integrity and truth; they stress the importance of facing facts and following them through to their logical conclusions. As they confront evidence about the intelligent design in our world, many find themselves agreeing with George Greenstein who asks:

"As we survey all the evidence, the thought insistently arises

## "Coincidences" in our cosmos

In recent years the parameters of our universe have been more sharply defined and analyzed than was ever imagined a few decades ago. Many scientists who do not call themselves Christian now readily admit that there are many "coincidences" in our cosmos which indicate that it has been designed.

### 1. Nuclear coupling

#### If weaker
The strong nuclear force coupling constant holds together the particles in the nucleus of an atom. If the strong nuclear force were slightly weaker, multi-proton nuclei would not hold together. This would result in hydrogen being the only element in the universe.

#### If stronger
If this force were slightly stronger, not only would hydrogen be rare in the universe, but the supply of the various life-essential elements heavier than iron (elements resulting from the fission of very heavy elements) would be insufficient. Either way, life would be impossible.

that some supernatural agency – or, rather, Agency – must be involved. Is it possible that suddenly, without intending to, we have stumbled upon scientific proof of the existence of a Supreme Being? Was it God who stepped in and so providentially crafted the cosmos for our benefit?"
*George Greenstein, American astronomer*

## 2. Electromagnetic coupling

The electromagnetic coupling constant binds electrons to protons in atoms. The characteristics of the orbits of electrons about atoms determines to what degree atoms will bond together to form molecules. If the electromagnetic coupling constant were slightly smaller, no electrons would be held in orbits about nuclei. If it were slightly larger, an atom could not "share" an electron orbit with other atoms. Either way, molecules, and hence life, would be impossible.

## 3. Electrons and protons

The ratio of electron to proton mass also determines the characteristics of the orbits of electrons about nuclei. A proton is 1836 times more massive than an electron. If the electron to proton mass ratio were slightly larger or slightly smaller, again, molecules would not form and life would be impossible.

## 4. Conclusion

These constants, and many similar constants, demonstrate why a growing number of physicists and astronomers have become convinced that the universe was not only divinely brought into existence but also divinely designed.

# The wonders of migration

### The argument

The one fact that naturalists must face is that the universe including our galaxy, our solar system, our earth, and all living creatures demonstrate some remarkable evidences of intelligent design.

### Chance or creation?

Taken separately, it is highly improbable that most characteristics of our world could have come about by random change. When taken together, the probability of life arriving on our planet by chance and random changes is so small as to be impossible.

The alternative to creation by chance is design by an intelligent Creator. This is a much more realistic explanation.

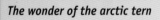

### The wonder of the arctic tern

The longest migration of any animal is the Arctic Tern.

Although the arctic tern is a small bird, only about 12–15 inches in length, weighing less than two pounds, it travels from the North Pole to the South Pole and back again each year.

#### Sterna paradisaea

Like gulls, terns are in the *Laridae* family. The Arctic Tern – *Sterna paradisaea* – has a white body with a smooth and rounded black head, short legs, and a slender, short, bright orange beak.

During breeding season, artic terns go to the polar regions above the fiftieth parallel in the Arctic Circle. Because of their migration timetable, Arctic Terns are in daylight longer than other birds.

### A miracle
Either way, one must admit that we are a product of a miracle. We are either a miracle of chance (as even an atheist has to concede) or a miracle of design (as Christians believe).

### Conclusion
The possibility that the universe was masterfully designed (instead of being a consequence of the forces of nature, plus time, plus chance) is not even allowed for by some scientists who have no place for a Designer in their thinking.

But Christians point to the wonders of our natural world and exclaim, "Yes, all of creation and all creatures are wonderfully made."

**"There is about us, if only we had eyes to see, a creation of such spectacular profusion, spendthrift richness, and absurd delight as to make us catch our breath in astonished wonder."** *Michael Mayne*

### The migration route
As the summer days get shorter, the Arctic Terns begin their migration south. They leave their breeding area only 90 days from the time they arrived in the Arctic.

From North America, they travel across the Atlantic Ocean to southern Europe, down the coast of Africa to the Antarctic.

### 22,000 miles a year
Their migration path is over 22,000 miles (35,000 km) each year. They travel about 11,000 miles each way between their breeding grounds in the Arctic and their winter home in the Antarctic.

No wonder the Arctic Tern has been called "the greatest traveler in the animal kingdom."

# What is the "Anthropic" principle?

## Anthropos

The anthropic principle derives its name from the Greek word for man, *anthropos*.

The anthropic principle focuses on how perfect the planet earth is, not only for life in general, but for human life in particular.

## "The most intriguing new scientific idea"

"The anthropic principle is the most intriguing new scientific idea of the last decade.

"… It is a massive piece of circumstantial evidence pointing to meaning and purpose in the universe.

"… The precise values of the speed of light, Planck's Constant, the mass of protons compared with neutrons, the total quantity of hydrogen and helium – all apparently unconnected conditions which have controlled every detail of the universe's development – seem to have been exactly programmed … all to one end: humanity.

"… If in the course of an experiment a scientist produced a result against odds this large, he certainly would not dismiss it as an accident. He would look for a cause."
*Clifford Longley in The [London] Times*

## Our "finely tuned" world

The universe and its physical laws depend upon fine-tuning. This is the insight of the anthropic principle.

Quite small changes in any of the basic physical laws would have a catastrophic effect on our universe. Its finely-tuned laws make the cosmos a one-in-a-trillion cosmos.

## Examples of fine tuning

If the power of gravity, the charge on the electron, or the nature of nuclear forces were even a little different from what they actually are, no life could exist on earth.

## A "designed" universe

The discovery of an overwhelming design in the universe is having a profound theological impact upon astronomers.

Fred Hoyle, Professor of Astronomy at Cambridge University from 1958 to 72, showed in 1956 how heavier elements can be built up from lighter ones in the interiors of stars. His conclusion in 1982 was:

"a super-intellect has monkeyed with physics, as well as with chemistry and biology."

Paul Davies, Professor of mathematical physics and professor of natural philosophy at Adelaide University, Australia, and also winner of the 1995 Templeton Foundation Prize for Progress in Religion, moved from promoting atheism in 1983 to conceding in 1984 that:

**"the laws [of physics] ... seem themselves to be the product of exceedingly ingenious design,"**

to testifying in 1988 that there:

**"is for me powerful evidence that there is something going on behind it all. The impression of design is overwhelming."**

### Quotation from a scientist/theologian

**"We do not live at the center of the universe, but neither do we live in just 'any old world.' Instead we live in a universe whose constitution is precisely adjusted to the narrow limits that alone would make it capable of being our home."**

*John Polkinghorne, President of Queens' College, Cambridge.*

# The design of our earth and solar system (1)

## Necessary parameters

Dozens of parameters of the universe have been identified that must be carefully fixed in order for any kind of conceivable life (not just life as we know it) to exist at any time in the history of the universe.

## World view and theology

If the universe is uncreated, eternally self-existent, or accidental then it has no purpose and, consequently, we have no purpose. Determinism rules. Morality and religion are ultimately irrelevant.

(Note: Determinism is the philosophical doctrine that every act or event is the

## Evidence of design

What is some of the evidence for the view that the sun-earth-moon system have been designed?

### 1. The "color" of the parent star

- **if redder:** photosynthetic response would be insufficient.
- **if bluer:** photosynthetic response would be insufficient.

During the process of photosynthesis green plants carbohydrates are synthesized from carbon dioxide and water using light as an energy source. Photosynthesis releases oxygen as a byproduct. Without photosynthesis humans would not have suitable air to breathe.

### 2. The distance from parent star

- **if farther:** the planet would be too cool for a stable water cycle.
- **if closer:** the planet would be too warm for a stable water cycle.

Without a stable water system it would be impossible for human life to develop. On average the Earth is 92,960,000 miles from the Sun. The closest it comes is 91,400,000 miles from the Sun and the furthest it goes from the Sun is 94,510,000 miles.

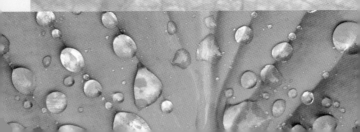

inevitable consequence of chance.)

If the universe is created and the creator is impersonal, then love, compassion, and care are merely illusions.

On the other hand, if the Creator is personal and created and designed planet Earth for a loving purpose, then these attributes and others such as beauty, altruism, mercy, and justice are real and meaningful.

### The facts of the world
"To be religious is to know that the facts of the world are not the end of the matter."
*Ludwig Wittgenstein, Austrian-born philosopher, (1889–1951)*

## 3. Inclination of orbit
• **if too great:** temperature differences on the planet would be too extreme.

The axis of the Earth is inclined at an angle of 23° to the plane of its orbit around the Sun. This gives rise to the seasons. If this angle was greatly changed, the temperatures on earth would become a great deal hotter or colder and plant life and animal life would not survive.

## 4. Orbital eccentricity
• **if too great:** seasonal temperatures differences would be too extreme.

The earth does not rotate around the sun in a perfect circle. The earth takes an elliptical path around the sun, the shape of an oval rather than a circle. This path is perfect for our present variation of the seasons. If the orbit of the Earth around the Sun greatly changed, the seasons as we know them would alter and many plants would not be able to survive.

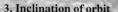

# The design of our earth and solar system (2)

## More evidence

There is yet more evidence to indicate that the sun-earth-moon system did not come about by chance but by design.

### 1. Thickness of the earth's crust

- **if thicker:** too much oxygen would be transferred from the atmosphere to the crust. Then there would not be enough oxygen left to permit the development of life as we know it.
- **if thinner:** volcanic and tectonic activity would be too great. There would be so much ash in the atmosphere along with so many earthquakes and tidal waves that human life would not develop.

### 2. Albedo (ratio of reflected light to total amount falling on surface)

- **if greater:** a runaway ice age would exist, preventing life.
- **if lesser:** there would be a runaway greenhouse effect, also preventing life.

Natural salt springs in Iceland.

### 3. Gravitational interaction with a moon

- **if greater:** tidal effects on the oceans, atmosphere, and rotational period would be too severe for life and as a result there would be catastrophic tidal waves.
- **if lesser:** orbital obliquity (incline or slope) changes would cause climatic instabilities. The regular seasons of the year as we know them – spring, summer, fall and winter would not be able to exist.

### 4. Water vapor level in atmosphere

- **if greater:** a runaway greenhouse effect would develop.
- **if lesser:** rainfall would be too meager to support advanced life on the land.

The Earth is surrounded by a 6,250 mile thick atmosphere made up of nitrogen, oxygen, argon, and carbon dioxide. If the water vapor level in the atmosphere greatly changed, the ozone layer, which is 12.5 miles above the Earth, would change and thus no longer be effective in blocking out the Sun's harmful ultraviolet rays.

### *Definite parameters*

Each of these parameters cannot exceed certain limits without disturbing a planet's capacity to support life.

### View of an award winning theoretical physicist

Freeman Dyson won the coveted Enrico Fermi Award in 1995. This award was named in honor of Enrico Fermi, the atomic pioneer. Each year the $100,000 award is given in recognition of "exceptional and altogether outstanding" scientific and technical achievement in atomic energy.

Dyson has written:
**"The more I examine the universe and the details of its architecture, the more evidence I find that the universe in some sense must have known that we were coming."**

He went on to write:
**"Technology without morality is barbarous; morality without technology is impotent."**

# The wonders of nature

## "I, the Lord, have created it"

"You heavens above, rain down
   righteousness;
let the clouds shower it down.
Let the earth open wide,
let salvation spring up,
let righteousness grow with it;
I, the Lord, have created it."
*Isaiah 45:8*

## Wonder

The word wonder is habitually
used by scientists to describe
their experiences and to justify
the great endeavor in which
they are engaged.

## Order in the world

Christians observe order in
our world and put this fact
alongside their belief that God
is One and that God is rational
and loving.

Christians do not despise
the material world. The
material world is good,
because it is created by God.
In Genesis chapter one, we
continually read:

"And God saw that it was
good." *Verses 10,12,18,21,25*

## Good old Earth

### Facts about our planet Earth

- Earth is the third planet from
  the Sun and the fifth largest:
- Earth's orbit: 89,760,000 miles
  from Sun
- Earth's diameter: 7,654 miles

### The Earth's chemical composition (by mass) is:

34.6% Iron
29.5% Oxygen
15.2% Silicon
12.7% Magnesium
2.4% Nickel
1.9% Sulfur
0.05% Titanium

- The Earth is the densest major
  body in the solar system.

### Water, water, everywhere

- 71% of the Earth's surface is
  covered with water.
- Earth is the only planet on
  which water can exist in liquid
  form on the surface. Liquid
  water is, of course, essential for
  life as we know it.
- The heat capacity of the oceans
  is very important in keeping the
  Earth's temperature relatively
  stable.
- Liquid water is responsible for
  most of the erosion and
  weathering of the Earth's
  continents, a process unique in
  the solar system today (though
  it may have occurred on Mars
  in the past).

### No pantheism

Pantheism, the system of belief that identifies God with the universe, is nowhere taught in the Bible. God is not in the trees and animals – he created them.

The popular pantheistic range of options are clearly rejected by Psalm 19. The heavens are God's servants – not God. God is beyond and above his creation.

### God's revelation of himself

God has revealed himself to all people through the wonders of nature. Everybody is aware of this, whether they care to admit it or not. This is very clearly taught in the Bible.

> "For since the creation of the world God's invisible qualities – his eternal power and divine nature – have been clearly seen, being understood from what has been made, so that men are without excuse."
>
> *Romans 1:20*

Another great commentary on the wonders of nature comes in the first chapter of Genesis:

> "God saw all that he had made, and it was very good."
>
> *Genesis 1:31*

### Intellectual beauty

> "The intellectual beauty of the order discovered by science is consistent with the physical world's having behind it the mind of the divine Creator."
>
> *John Polkinghorne, President of Queens' College, Cambridge.*

### Sense of wonder

> "A man who has lost his sense of wonder is a man dead."
>
> *William of St Thierry (1085–1148)*

### Quotation from a philosopher/statesman

> "I had rather believe all the legends of Aesop and all the fables of the Talmud than believe that this universal frame is without a mind."
>
> *Francis Bacon*

# Look at the stars

### The starry host

We live on a small planet which circles one star.

Our galaxy is just one among many millions of galaxies in the universe. We are part of the enormous Milky Way galaxy which is made up of 200 billion stars. These stars are spread across 150,000 light years and are 1,000 light years thick.

> **"Put three grains of sand inside a vast cathedral, and the cathedral will be more closely packed with sand than space is with stars."**
>
> *Sir James Jeans, 1877–1946, English astonomer*

### Distant stars

There are millions of other galaxies beyond the Milky Way.

Astronomical telescopes have detected objects which are believed to be so remote that it has taken their light the equivalent of 10 billion years to reach us. Light travels at 186,000 miles per second.

The Sun is so far away from us – 93 million miles – that it takes 8 minutes for its light to reach us. But by astronomical standards the sun is very close to us.

Pluto, on average, is forty times as far from the Sun as we are.

### The moon

> **"The moon marks off the seasons,**
> **and the sun knows when to go down."**
> *Psalm 104:19*

If the earth's moon was larger its gravitational pull would cause massive tidal waves which would threaten our existence.

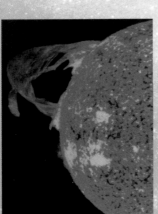

### Jupiter

Jupiter plays a vital role in our solar system. Jupiter is so large and has such a strong gravitational pull that large meteors which might have otherwise bombarded the earth are attracted to Jupiter as if it were a magnet.

### God made the stars

The conclusions that a believer in a Designer draws from looking at a star-studded sky are:

- "God did this."
- "God is unimaginably powerful."
- "Here is no random combining of atoms."
- "This is the work of the Creator God."
- "How wonderful our God is. He created every twinkling star."

One of God's most faithful Old Testament servants wrote: **"You alone are the Lord. You made the heavens, even the highest heavens, and all the starry host ..."** *Nehemiah 9:6*

### "How do you know there is a God?"

**"The heavens declare the glory of God;**
**the skies proclaim the work of his hands."**
*Psalm 19:1*

This psalm states that the glories of nature point to a God of creation, and this evidence should be considered by non-Christians.

### The sun

"How do you know there is a God?" an atheist asked a Bedouin.

He replied, "How do I know that it was a man and not a camel that went past my tent last night? I know him by his tracks." Then, pointing to the sun, he added, "There is the track of a God."

### The stars

During the French revolution, an atheist tried to threaten a God-fearer by saying: "We'll pull all your church steeples down, and destroy the memory of your God."

The God-fearer replied, "You can't pull the stars down."

# The Bible is not against science

### A literal interpretation

Belief in a "God of the gaps" comes from a literal interpretation of poetic expressions in the Bible which talk about God controlling the world. If we are to understand the Bible correctly, we must recognize the type of literature that is being used in different parts of the Bible.

There are distinctions between narrative, poetry, proverb, parable, and history. If we do not take this into account, we are liable to fall into many traps and contradictions.

### Silly arguments

Some people have wasted their energy by arguing about things like whether the Bible is right when it says that God sends the rains.

"I will send rain on the earth," *Genesis 7:4.*

This doesn't mean that God's hand carries the cloud along. Nor does it mean that God blows the wind along! It simply means that God is ultimately responsible for the rain.

### Anthropomorphism

In the Bible God is often spoken of in human terms. The psalmist describes God creating the heavens with his fingers:

"When I consider your heavens,
the work of your fingers,
the moon and the stars,
which you have set in place,
what is man that you are mindful of him? ..." *Psalm 8:3-4*

The prophet Jeremiah talks of God's arm being responsible for creation:

"With my great power and outstretched arm I made the earth and its people and the animals that are on it, and I give it to anyone I please." *Jeremiah 27:5*

Anthropomorphism is a literary device. Christians rather than non-Christians have been guilty of interpreting figurative Bible verses literally.

### Science and the Bible

For Christians, God is the God of truth. The same God is the "author" of nature and the "author" of the Bible.

## Discrepancies

But there are apparent discrepancies between what are hailed as "the assured findings of science" and the traditional teaching of the Bible.

What is a modern Christian to do about such supposed discrepancies?

There are only two avenues to pursue.

- Scientists must rigorously examine any implications which have been drawn from their discoveries.
- Christians must carefully scrutinize their own interpretation of the Bible.

## Science and theology

Scientists and theologians are looking at the same data from two different angles. They are observing and describing different facets of the same diamond.

Science and the Bible offer complementary answers to many questions

## Quote from a scientist

"It is the contention of the Christian that, in order to do full justice to the totality of his experience, he finds it necessary to see and interpret the over-all pattern of his experience not only in biochemical, physiological or psychological terms, but also in religious terms."
*Malcolm Jeeves, former Professor of Psychology at St Andrew's University, Scotland, and Adelaide University, Australia.*

## Creator God

"It is I who made the earth and created mankind upon it. My own hands stretched out the heavens;
I marshaled their starry hosts."
*Isaiah 45:12*

# Three cheers for Galileo

## Galileo

The treatment Galilei Galileo (1564–1642) received at the hands of church officials continues to make people think that science is somehow a threat to Christianity and that Christians are opposed to science.

Galileo demonstrated that the earth is not the center of our universe. Yet, this was seen as heresy by the Roman Catholic hierarchy of his day and he was tried and condemned to house arrest by the Roman Inquisition.

A literal and mistaken interpretation of such Bible verses as Psalm 33:9, "[the earth] stood firm", and,

**"Who laid the foundations of the earth, that it should not be removed for ever"**
*Psalm 104:5, King James Version,*

was used against Galileo. People were led to believe, as an article of faith, that the earth was the center of the world and that the sun revolved around the earth.

## The earth as the center of the universe

As far as our solar system is concerned, it is claimed that some biblical references are scientifically inaccurate since they seem to describe the sun as revolving around the earth.

**"It [the sun] rises at one end of the heavens and makes it circuit to the other ..."**
*Psalm 19:6*

However, we must keep in mind that even in our modern, scientific culture we use the phrases "sunrise" and "sunset", without being accused of scientific inaccuracies. They are simply everyday expressions that most people understand.

When the Bible speaks about scientific matters it usually does so in everyday language. The sun "rises" and the heavens are "above" us.

## Copernicus

Nicolaus Copernicus (1473–1543) put forward the heliocentric theory of planetary movement in which, in contrast to the views held earlier, the sun and not the earth is at the center of the universe and other planets, including the earth, revolve around the sun. In light of this, the words in Psalm 19:6 about the sun rising at one end of the heavens and making its circuit to the other might appear to be senseless. However we know today that although the sun does not revolve around the earth, it does move on a predestined path.

## An unknown center

We now know that our sun is no more fixed in space than the earth is. It is revolving around an unknown center of the Milky Way galaxy. Therefore, all motion is relative motion, and the best way to describe it is to arbitrarily select a point of assumed zero velocities and measure all velocities relative to that point.

So in relation to astronomy the Bible is found to be accurate.

## Reading the Bible

As we read the Bible we are struck by the fact that although it is not a book of science, it enumerates numerous scientific facts that were included there long before their discovery. All these were written in the Bible many centuries ago. They reveal the nature of God and his creations.

## The earth is the Lord's

"The earth is the Lord's,
    and everything in it,
the world, and all who live
    in it ..."
Psalm 24:1

# Has evolution replaced our need for God?

## Alan Isaacs

In *The Survival of God in the Scientific Age*, Dr Alan Isaacs writes:

"**The properties of the ultimate particles which constitute the material universe ... spontaneously interact in certain ways and organize themselves (without apparent intervention) into units of increasing complexity. Eventually after a sufficient number of stages of organization, these attributes include those associated with life, thought and consciousness. This process appears to be self-actuating, self-perpetuating and reproducible. At no stage therefore, is it necessary to postulate a divine intelligence.**"

**Conclusion:** look on the world as a closed mechanistic system, and you will find no room for God in it.

As a result, the so-called intellectuals of the world have written off God as a non-essential.

## The theory of evolution

Some people have suggested that the theory of evolution can be extended to provide a complete answer to the origin of all life replacing any need for God.

**Before you accept this theory, there are two important questions you should ask.**

1. How was the first life-form produced?
2. How did the first life-form manage to develop into all the life-forms we now see?

## The origin of life

Clearly it is only living, self-replicating organisms (those that can reproduce) that can evolve. So we have to ask the question – where did the first self-replicating organism come from? Even if particles can react together, where did the particles come from in the first place? In other words, how did life begin?

If there is no God we have to say that this happened by chance. But this solution is far from being a straightforward explanation.

### The chance theory

If we decide that the first life to occur was a self-replicating cell, we have accepted that something extremely improbable happened. The probability of the spontaneous production of just the 200 enzymes necessary for such a cell has been calculated as 1 in $10^{40,000}$. That is 1 in 10 with 40,000 zeros after it.

### Sir Fred Hoyle

The British astronomer, Sir Fred Hoyle, who founded the world-famous Institute of Theoretical Astronomy, states concerning the possibility of spontaneous generation of life:

> "The chance that higher life forms might have emerged in this way is comparable with the chance that a tornado sweeping through a junk-yard might assemble a Boeing 747 from the materials therein."

A Boeing 747 is a collection of 4.5 million non-flying parts, arranged in an intricate design such that it can fly.

A typical cell contains several billion non-living molecules such as proteins, DNA, and RNA all arranged in intricate design. According to Denton a typical cell contains ten million million atoms. Its life depends on the integrated activity of tens or even hundreds of thousands of different proteins.

### A biologist's view

> "The probability of life originating from accident is comparable to the probability of a dictionary resulting from an explosion in a printing works." *Edward Conklin*

### Statistically, spontaneous generation is impossible

Dr. Duane Gish states that the probability of a protein of only 50 amino acids forming would be 1 in $10^{65}$. The simplest "living" organism would have at least 400 amino acids.

> "Any honest man, armed with all the knowledge available to us now, could only state that in some sense, the origin of life appears at the moment to be almost a miracle." *Francis Crick*

### The God hypothesis

To believe that our universe happened all by chance is to take a huge leap of faith.

To believe in God does require faith, but it is not unreasonable.

> "In the beginning you laid the foundations of the earth." *Psalm 102:25*

# If science were king

## What if ...?

If the universe is created and the creator is impersonal, then where do love, compassion, and care fit in?

On the other hand, if the Creator is personal, then these attributes and others such as beauty, altruism, mercy, and justice are real and meaningful.

## Glory be to atheism

The following "Hymn to atheism" comes from the pen of one of the most celebrated atheistic philosophers of the twentieth century.

56

> "A FREE MAN'S WORSHIP
> That man is the product of causes which had no prevision of the end they were achieving, that his origin, growth, hopes and fears, loves and beliefs are but the outcome of accidental collocation of atoms; that no fire, no heroism ... can preserve an individual life beyond the grave ... that the whole temple of man's achievement must inevitably be buried beneath the debris of a universe in ruins – all these things, if not quite beyond dispute, are yet so nearly certain that no philosophy which rejects them can hope to stand."
> Bertrand Russell

## No more need for God

For some scientists today the advances in space exploration and in medical science make the "God hypothesis" seem rather old-fashioned and unnecessary.

Sir Richard Gregory, a former Editor of *Nature*, wrote the following epitaph for himself.

> "My grandfather preached the gospel of Christ,
> My father preached the gospel of Socialism,
> I preach the gospel of Science."

## No novel idea

Science's quest to remove God from the scene is no new idea. The free thinkers at the Congress of Liege in 1865 concluded,

> "Science does not deny God:, she makes him unnecessary."
> "Men have become like gods ... Science offers us total mastery over our environment and over our destiny." *Edmund Leach*

### The horrors of war

Reflect on the atrocities of Auschwitz. Bertrand Russell stated:

> "Science can enable our grandchildren to live the good life, by giving them knowledge, self-control, and characters productive of harmony rather than strife."

Russell said this before the carnage of the two World Wars of the twentieth century. History demonstrates that the philosophy of a merely evolutionary mechanistic world-view is no help in controlling man's inhumanity to man.

### What is the result of rejecting God?

A German theologian points out the fallacy of a mechanistic view of the universe.

> "The feeling for the personal and the human which is the fruit of faith may outlive for a time the death of the roots from which it has grown. But this cannot last very long. As a rule the decay of religion works out in the second generation as moral rigidity and in the third generation as the breakdown of all morality. Humanity without religion has never been a historical force capable of resistance. Dehumanization results."
>
> *Emil Brunner*

### Science and faith in God

> "If you think strongly enough, you will be forced by Science to believe in God."
>
> *Lord Kelvin*

# Thinking, communicating, and seeing

### The human brain
It is unthinkable to assume that blind chance formed the human brain with its 12 billion brain cells and its $10^{15}$ connections, which according to Isaac Asimov is "the most complex and orderly arrangement of matter in the universe."

The human brain has greater reasoning powers than the strongest computer. The electrical activity in our brains goes on twenty-four hours a day and our brains use enough electricity to power a ten-watt lightbulb.

### Good communications
Our bodies have more than 12,000 million nerve cells. They are linked to each other by more than 10 million million connections.

### Communication between elephants
Low frequency calls can be heard up to 5 miles away by other elephants. About two thirds of such calls are too low for human ears to detect.

### Communication between whales
Whales can hear the "songs" from another whale over 100 miles away. While sound waves travel through air at 1,120 feet per second, they travel much faster through water, at the rate of 5,000 feet per second.

### Sharp-eyed sharks
Sharks' eyes focus light three times more efficiently than human eyes can.

### Insects' eyes
Insects have eyes that can detect polarized light. This enables them to find the position of the sun.

A fly's eye is made up of over 5,000 optical units. Compound eyes, which some shellfish also have, enable a nearly 360 degrees of field of view, so they can see in all directions at once.

Some insects can detect a movement that only lasts for one-thousandth of a second. Human eyes cannot detect the 100 wing beats per second of some humming birds, but a number of insects have no difficulty in detecting this.

## Rods and cones

Rods and cones are the names given to the two types of light receptors possessed by humans. Rods can only detect grey and shades of grey. Cones can distinguish between colors. Each of our eyes have about 125 million rods and 7 million cones.

## What conclusion do you come to?

- We stagger as we think about how we are made.
- We fall to our knees in wonder before our Creator God.
- We are overwhelmed by sheer bewilderment.
- We conclude: "Only the All-powerful God could have created us like that!"

## Wonderfully made

When we consider our human bodies, we say with the Psalmist,

"I praise you because I am fearfully and wonderfully made; your works are wonderful, I know that full well." *Psalm 139:14*

And the Christian agrees with Isaac Newton when he said,

"In the absence of any other proof, the thumb alone would convince me of God's existence."

## The study of science

"If the study of science teaches one anything, it is that the world is full of surprises – that reality is stranger than we could have imagined. Who would have supposed that the clear and reliable world of everyday experience is made of subatomic constituents whose behavior is cloudy and fitful? … I used quantum theory everyday in my working life as a theoretical physicist. Invented to describe atoms, it is now applied with great success to account for the behavior of quarks and gluons, which are at least a hundred million times smaller than atoms. Yet a great paradox remains. We still do not understand quantum theory fully. The measurement problem (how the fitful quantum world and the reliable everyday world interlock) is still a matter of unresolved dispute."

Serious Talk, *John Polkinghorne, SCM, vii-viii.*

(John Polkinghorne spent most of his adult life working as a theoretical physicist. He is now an Anglican clergyman and President of Queens' College, Cambridge.)

# A galaxy of testimonies

## Galileo

Galileo and Copernicus remained devout Christian men, convinced that their work glorified God, despite the constant obscurantism of the Catholic Church of the day.

"Since the Holy Ghost did not intend to teach us whether heaven moves or stands still ... nor whether the earth is located at its center or off to one side, then so much the less was it intended to settle for us any other conclusion of the same kind. ... Now if the Holy Spirit has purposely neglected to teach us propositions of this sort as irrelevant to the highest goal (that is, to our salvation), how can anyone affirm that it is obligatory to take side on them? ... I would say here something that was heard from an ecclesiastic of the most eminent degree: 'The intention of the Holy Ghost is to teach us how one goes to heaven, not how heaven goes.'"
Galileo

## Isaac Newton

Isaac Newton wrote his *Principia* in the assurance that "this world could originate from nothing but the perfectly free will of God." He is said to have spent more time in Bible study than in scientific research.

He once said,
"There is but one God the Father of whom are all things and we in him and one Lord Jesus Christ by whom are all things and we by him."

## Robert Boyle

Robert Boyle, one of the founders of the Royal Society, was a sincere Christian and endowed a lectureship for

"proving the Christian religion against notorious infidels."

## Simpson

James Young Simpson, 1811–70, the first surgeon to use chloroform as an anaesthetic, was once asked what his greatest discovery was. He replied:

"It was not chloroform. My greatest discovery has been to know that I am a sinner and that I could be saved by the grace of God."

### The testimony of an environmentalist

"It is indeed a sobering thought that the early writings of the Jewish people [the Old Testament] encompass all the basic recommendations of world conservation strategy."

*Professor David Bellamy*

### The testimony of an historian

"Historically, religion came first and science grew out of religion. Science has never superseded religion, and it is my expectation that it never will supersede it."

*Arnold Toynbee*

### The testimony of a quantum theorist

"Religion and natural science are fighting a joint battle in an incessant never relaxing crusade against skepticism and against dogmatism, against disbelief and against superstition, and the rallying cry in this crusade has always been, and always will be: 'On to God.'"

*Max Planck, Nobel Prize winner*

### The testimony of a physicist

"Science without religion is lame, religion without science is blind."

*Albert Einstein*

### Is life meaningless? Two writers give their testimony

"I was just thinking ... that here we are, all of us, eating and drinking, to preserve our previous existence, and that there's nothing, nothing, absolutely no reason for existing."

*Jean-Paul Sartre*

"If one puts aside the existence of God ... one has to make up one's mind what is the meaning and use of life. Now the answer is plain, but so unpalatable that most men will not face it. There is no reason for life, and life has no meaning."

*Somerset Maugham*

# Look at the flowers

### Creator God

Either the God of the Bible is the creator of the universe or he is not. The Bible tells us that God created the heavens and the earth. God then made all life that lives on earth, culminating in the creation of humankind.

### God speaks and it happens

Then God said, "Let the land produce vegetation: seed-bearing plants and trees on the land that bear fruit with seed in it, according to their various kinds." And it was so. The land produced vegetation: plants bearing seed according to their various kinds and trees bearing fruit with seed in it according to their kinds. And God saw that it was good.
*Genesis 1:11-12*

### The sunflower

The humble sunflower is a very popular flower as it is so often grown by children. It is very easy to cultivate and most varieties thrive in poor soil. It is rarely attacked by pests and common varieties grow up to 12 feet or even up to 18 feet tall.

**Sunflower quick facts**
- The tallest sunflower grown on record was 25 feet tall and was grown in the Netherlands.
- The largest sunflower head on record measured 32 inches across its widest point and was grown in Canada.
- The shortest mature sunflower on record was just over 2 inches tall and was grown in Oregon using the Bonsai technique.

### *Helianthus annuus*

Sunflowers are of the genus *Helianthus*, coming from the Greek words *helios* for "sun" and *anthos* for "flower." Sunflowers thrive on the sun and their heads follow the sun during the day.

**Ray flowers and disc flowers**
The simple beauty of a sunflower becomes more complicated with closer inspection. The sunflower head contains two types of flowers: the ray flowers and the disk flowers.
- The petals of the ray flowers are broad-based and ring the outer edge of the flower head. They serve as attention-getters waving to nearby insects and luring them to the flower center.

### The Christian response

- One field of wild flowers blows the mind.
- It's just not good enough to say that our world just "evolved" by some "chance collocation of atoms," as atheists like Bertrund Russell would have us believe.
- Every flower trumpets the glory of its Creator.
- God made our world and everything in it.

- The center flowers, called disk flowers, are tubular in shape. To be fertilized they require pollen from another sunflower plant. The insects cross-pollinate the disk flowers which then develop into seeds.

### Sunflower seeds

The seeds are very high in many minerals, vitamins, and essential acids.

- The main nutrients are: protein, thiamine, vitamin E, iron, phosphorous, potassium, calcium, linoleic acid, and oleic acid (two essential fatty acids).
- Sunflowers are in the same protein league as beef and are higher in iron than any other food except egg yolks and liver.

### Creator and Sustainer

God is not only the Savior of the world, he is the Creator and Sustainer of the world. By looking at nature we can glimpse a snapshot of the glory of the Creator God.

### Heaven breaking through

As William Law put it: the Christian sees,

> "nothing else but heaven breaking through the veil of this world,"

### The stupendous sunflower

Every part of the plant is useful:
- the leaves form a cattle-food
- the stems contain a fibre for making paper.
- the seeds are rich in oil
- the flowers contain a yellow dye

### The Mammoth Sunflower

The Mammoth or Giant Sunflower which comes from Russia is called the Russian Sunflower and it produces 15-inch-wide heads containing 2,000 seeds.

One acre of Russian Sunflowers yields about 50 bushels of seeds while it furnishes 50 gallons of oil and 150 lbs. of oil-cake.

A Designer has truly designed a unique, wonderful, and useful flower.

# Giving an answer

### A Christian apologetic

The English word "apologetics" comes from the Greek word *apologia* which refers to a verbal defense or an answer. It is the word translated "answer" in 1 Peter 3:15 and is used seven other times in the New Testament. Thus, apologetics refers to the defense of the Christian faith against all intellectual attacks.

Apologetics can include scientific, theological, and philosophical arguments in support of God, the Bible, and the Christian faith.

### Peter's advice

"But in your hearts set apart Christ as Lord. Always be prepared to give an answer to everyone who asks you to give the reason for the hope that you have. But do this with gentleness and respect."
*1 Peter 3:15*

Christians are commanded to defend the Christian faith.

### Jude

Jude wrote his letter to encourage Christians to expose the false teaching and immoral behavior of some ungodly people who had attached themselves to the Christian fellowship.

"I felt I had to write and urge you to contend for the faith that was once for all delivered to the saints." *Jude 3*

### Paul

Paul advises the Colossian Christians about the way in which they should speak up for their faith in Christ.

"Let your conversation be always full of grace, seasoned with salt, so that you may know how to answer everyone." *Colossians 4:6*

The early Christians, and Paul in particular, spent a good part of his ministry defending the Christian faith. See Acts 4:33; 14:15-17; 26:9-22; Romans 1:20; 1 Corinthians 15:1-8.